15
Fun and Easy Games for Young Learners
READING

**Reproducible, Easy-to-Play Learning Games
That Help Kids Build Essential Reading Skills**

BY SUSAN JULIO

SCHOLASTIC
PROFESSIONAL BOOKS

NEW YORK • TORONTO • LONDON • AUCKLAND • SYDNEY
• MEXICO CITY • NEW DELHI • HONG KONG • BUENOS AIRES

Cover and interior design by Susan Kass
Illustrations by Teresa Anderko

ISBN 0-439-20255-8
Copyright © 2001 by Susan Julio
All rights reserved.
Printed in the U.S.A.

Table of Contents

About This Book

Young children learn by playing. During early childhood, as students begin to understand the foundational strategies and skills that will enable them to communicate through writing, speaking, listening, and reading in the future, they need to experience the fun and enjoyment of language. Language games can help create that experience. The goal of this book is to enable teachers to supplement and reinforce their basic language arts program with easy-to-make, easy-to-play games that will help students practice phonemic awareness, letter names, sound-letter correspondences, decoding skills, high-frequency vocabulary, word-attack strategies, and comprehension skills.

The games presented in this book are designed to be useful in a wide variety of classroom situations. In addition, you may be able to find ways to adapt the games to fit the different learning needs of your students.

Each learning game identifies the language arts skill being reinforced, suggests the number of players, states a game objective, lists materials needed, provides easy-to-follow directions on how to play the game, and offers a variation for expanded game use.

How to Use This Book

In this book, you'll find reproducible game boards, cards, number cubes, spinners, and markers. To ensure durability, photocopy the game pieces on card stock and laminate. To assemble the number cubes, cut along the dotted lines, then fold along the solid lines and glue where indicated.

Keep the pieces together in large, resealable bags or folders. Label the bag or folder with the name of the game, the skill it reinforces, the number of players, and the list of materials inside.

As you introduce each new game, play it with your students or assist them as they play. You may want to make transparencies of the game board and/or game pieces to display on an overhead projector to demonstrate the game or play with the entire class. You may also want to teach the game to several students and have them teach it to their classmates. Invite students to play the games during language arts and/or center time. Consider sending games home to encourage family involvement.

Who Goes First?

- **Games for 2 players:** Encourage students to take turns going first or roll a number cube to determine who goes first.
- **Games for 2 or more players:** Have students roll a number cube to determine who goes first, second, and so on.

Socks

Skill
Visual discrimination

Players
2 to 4

Object
To match pairs of socks and accumulate the most pairs

Materials
• 2 sets of Sock cards (page 6)

How to Play

1. Shuffle the Sock cards and place them facedown on a table in rows.

2. Players take turns turning over two cards at a time. If the socks on the cards match, the player keeps the pair.

3. Play continues until all the socks are gone. The player with the most pairs wins.

Variation:
Remove one sock and play Odd Sock Out. Deal the cards to each player. Players take turns drawing a card from the person to the left. Players put down all pairs. The player with the remaining odd Sock card wins.

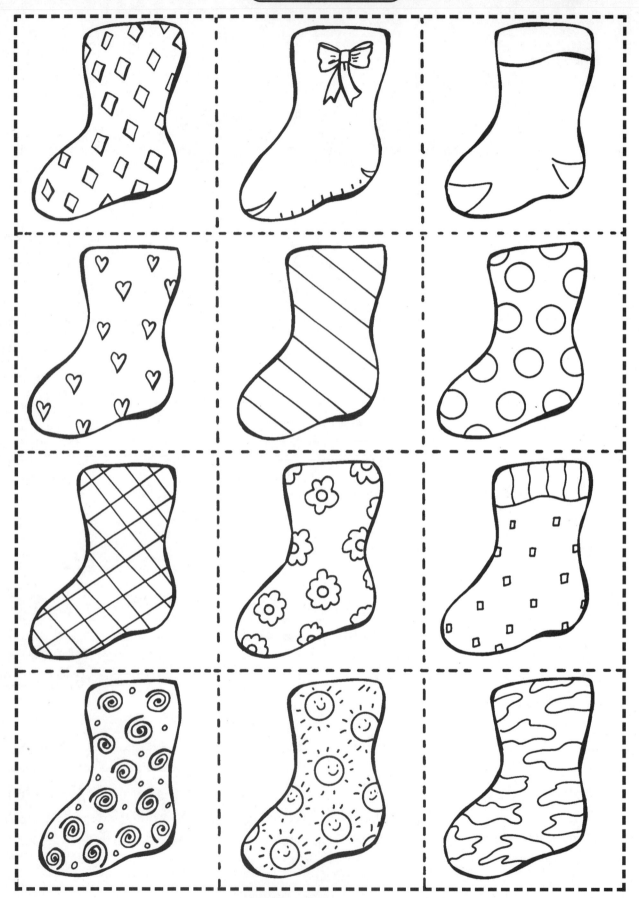

White Elephant

Skill
Identifying color words

Players
2 to 4

Object
To match Elephants of the same color and avoid being left holding the White Elephant at the end of play

Materials
- 2 sets of Elephant cards* (page 8)

*Make only one copy of the white Elephant card.

How to Play

1. Color and cut out the Elephant cards. Shuffle the deck and deal five cards to each player. Stack the rest of the deck facedown on the table.

2. Players take turns either drawing a card from the deck or choosing a card from the hand of the player on the right. If a player makes a match, he or she places the pair faceup on the table.

3. Play continues until all pairs are matched. The person with the white Elephant loses.

Variation:
Make an extra white Elephant card and place all the cards facedown on a table for Concentration.

White · Orange · Gray · Purple · Pink · Yellow · Red · Blue · Brown · Green · Black · Tan

What's the Scoop?

Skill
Alphabetizing

Players
2

Object
To be the first player to put words in alphabetical order

Materials
- 26 Scoop cards (page 10)
- Cone for each player (page 10)
- Number cube (page 10)

How to Play

1. Write one word on each Scoop, using the word list below or your own vocabulary words.

2. Shuffle the Scoops and stack them facedown on a table. Deal three Scoops to each player, keeping the cards facedown in front of them. Give each player a Cone.

3. Players take turns rolling the number cube. If the cube lands on a number, both players take that number of Scoops from the stack. If the cube lands on the Cone, both players turn over their Scoops and place them on their Cones in alphabetical order from top to bottom.

4. The first player to get his or her Scoops in the correct order wins. Scoops may be reshuffled and the game played again.

Variation:
For a more challenging game, use words that have the same first letter.

Word List:

• apple	• egg	• ice	• me	• queen	• up	• yellow
• ball	• fly	• jump	• nest	• rainbow	• violet	• zebra
• cat	• go	• kite	• on	• sit	• water	
• dog	• hop	• lamp	• pan	• ten	• X ray	

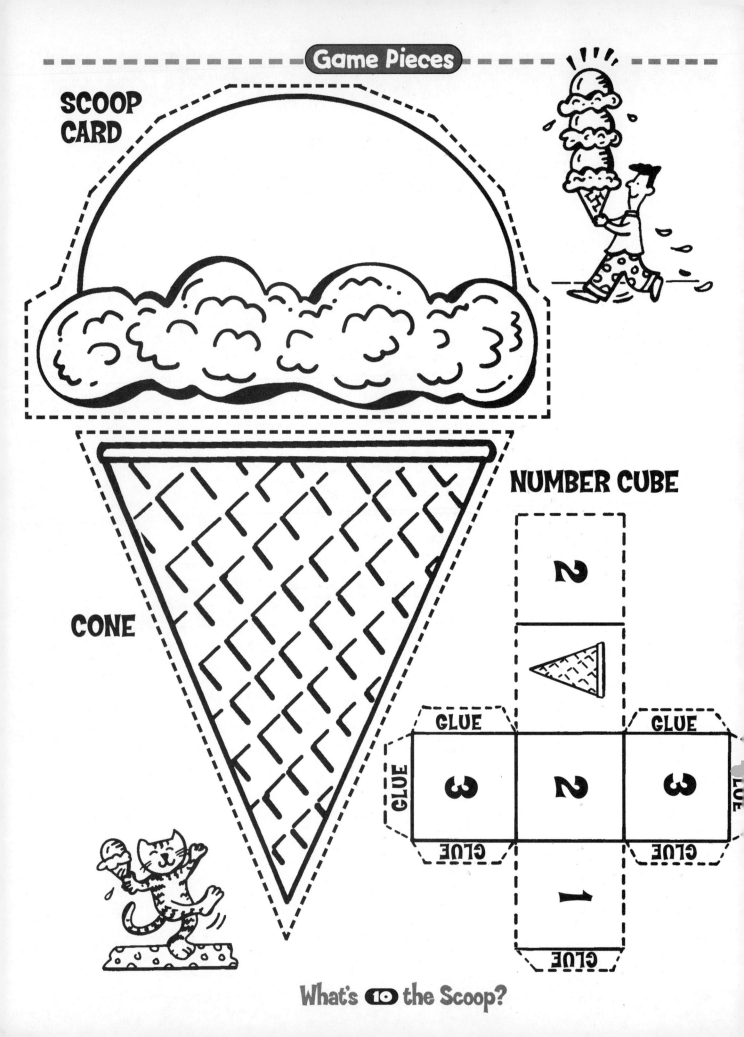

SCOOP CARD

CONE

NUMBER CUBE

2

GLUE
GLUE
3
2
3
GLUE
GLUE
1
GLUE

Gum Ball Bingo

Skill
Matching uppercase and lowercase letters

Players
2 to 4, plus a Letter Caller

Object
To match uppercase letters on the Letter cards with lowercase letters on the game board and be the first to color in all the Gum Ball spaces

Materials
- Gum Ball Bingo game board for each player (page 12)
- Letter cards (page 13)
- Crayons

How to Play

1. Write any 10 lowercase letters in random order inside the circles on each Gum Ball Bingo game board.

2. Shuffle the Letter cards and stack them facedown next to the Letter Caller. Give each player a game board and a crayon.

3. The Letter Caller draws a Letter card, reads it aloud, and shows it to the players. Players who have the matching lowercase letter written on their game board color it in.

4. The first player to correctly color in all his or her spaces calls out, "Gum Ball!" and wins.

Variation:
Enlarge the game board to accommodate 26 circles. Make brightly colored gum ball circles with uppercase letters and distribute them to each player. Display an object and have the player with the same beginning letter come and place their gum ball circle on the game board.

Gum Ball Bingo

A	B	C	D
E	F	G	H
I	J	K	L
M	N	O	P
Q	R	S	T
U	V	W	X
Y	Z		

I'm All Ears

Skill

Auditory discrimination

Players

2 to 4, plus a Caller

Object

To match read-aloud words with written words on the game board and be the first player to cover the game board

Materials

- Cornfield game board for each player (page 15)
- 9 Corn markers for each player (page 15)
- Word cards (page 16)

How to Play

1. Using the word list below, write nine words in each Cornfield game board in random order. For example, for the first game board, pick nine words from Card 1 and write them in the spaces.

2. Give each player a Cornfield game board and nine markers. Shuffle the Word cards and stack them next to the Caller.

3. The Caller draws a Word card and reads the word aloud. The player with that word on his or her game board covers that space with a Corn marker. The first player to cover all his or her spaces calls out "I'm All Ears!" and wins.

Variation:

Make up new word cards using consonant blends, such as *church* and *cheese, sheep* and *ship*, etc.

Word List:

Card 1:

hat hay mat may rat ray bat bay sit sat

Card 2:

dad Dan mad man pad pan tan ten red ran

Card 3:

bad ban cad can fad fan fed bed log dog

Card 4:

lad lap Tad tap sad sap tip sip set let

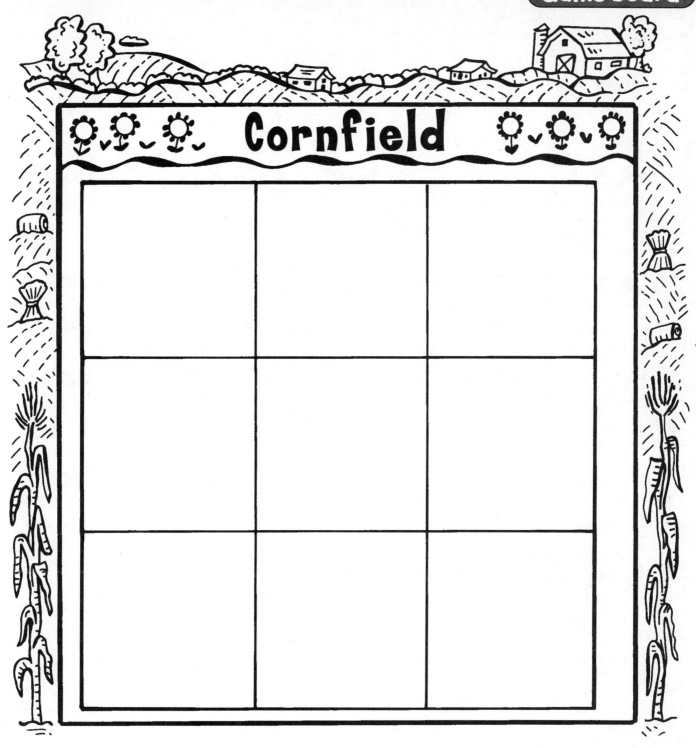

Cornfield

CORN MARKERS

hat	hay	mat	may	log
rat	ray	bat	bay	dog
sit	sat	dad	Dan	lad
mad	man	pad	pan	lap
tan	ten	red	ran	Tad
bad	ban	cad	can	tap
fad	fan	fed	bed	sad
let	sap	tip	sip	set

Butterfly Collector

Skill
Identifying beginning and ending sounds

Players
2 to 4

Object
To form words by adding a vowel between beginning and ending consonants, and collect the most Butterfly cards

Materials
- Butterfly cards (pages 18–19)
- Vowel cube (page 19)

How to Play

1. Spread the Butterfly cards faceup on a table.

2. Players take turns rolling the vowel cube. If a player can place the cube on the space on a Butterfly card to make a word, he or she keeps the card. For example, if a player rolls an "a," he or she might put the cube in the space between "c" and "p" to form the word "cap."

3. Play continues until all the cards are gone. The player with the most cards wins.

Variation:
To make the game more challenging, color the Butterfly cards two or more colors (use only one color per butterfly). Players try to collect only Butterflies of one color, such as all blues, all greens, or all reds.

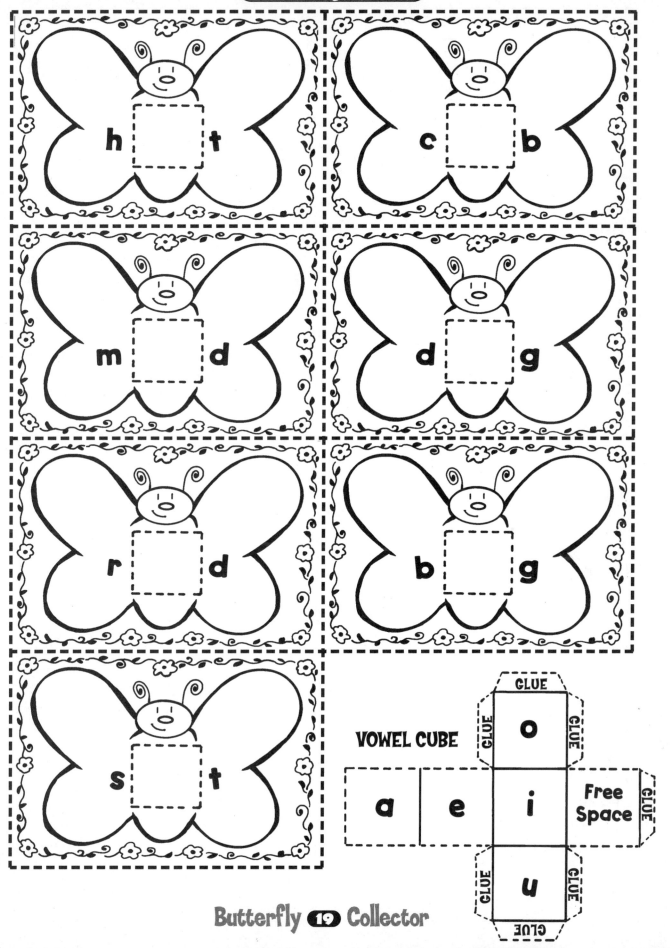

h   t

c   b

m   d

d   g

r   d

b   g

s   t

VOWEL CUBE

GLUE

o

GLUE

GLUE

a   e   i   Free Space

GLUE

GLUE   GLUE

u

GLUE

Regatta

Skill
Identifying long-vowel sounds

Players
2 to 4

Object
To match long-vowel sounds on the Word cards with the vowels
on the game board and be the first boat to cross the finish line

Materials
- Regatta game board (page 21)
- Boat markers (page 22)
- Word cards (pages 22–23)

How to Play

1. Shuffle the Word cards and stack them facedown next to the game board.

2. Each player chooses a Boat marker and places it on START. Players take turns drawing a card and moving to the nearest space that matches the vowel sound in the word on the card.

3. Players continue drawing cards and moving along the game board until one player reaches FINISH and wins. (Note: Cards may be reshuffled and drawn again during play if needed.)

Variation:
Create new game cards to help introduce vocabulary words with short-vowel sounds.

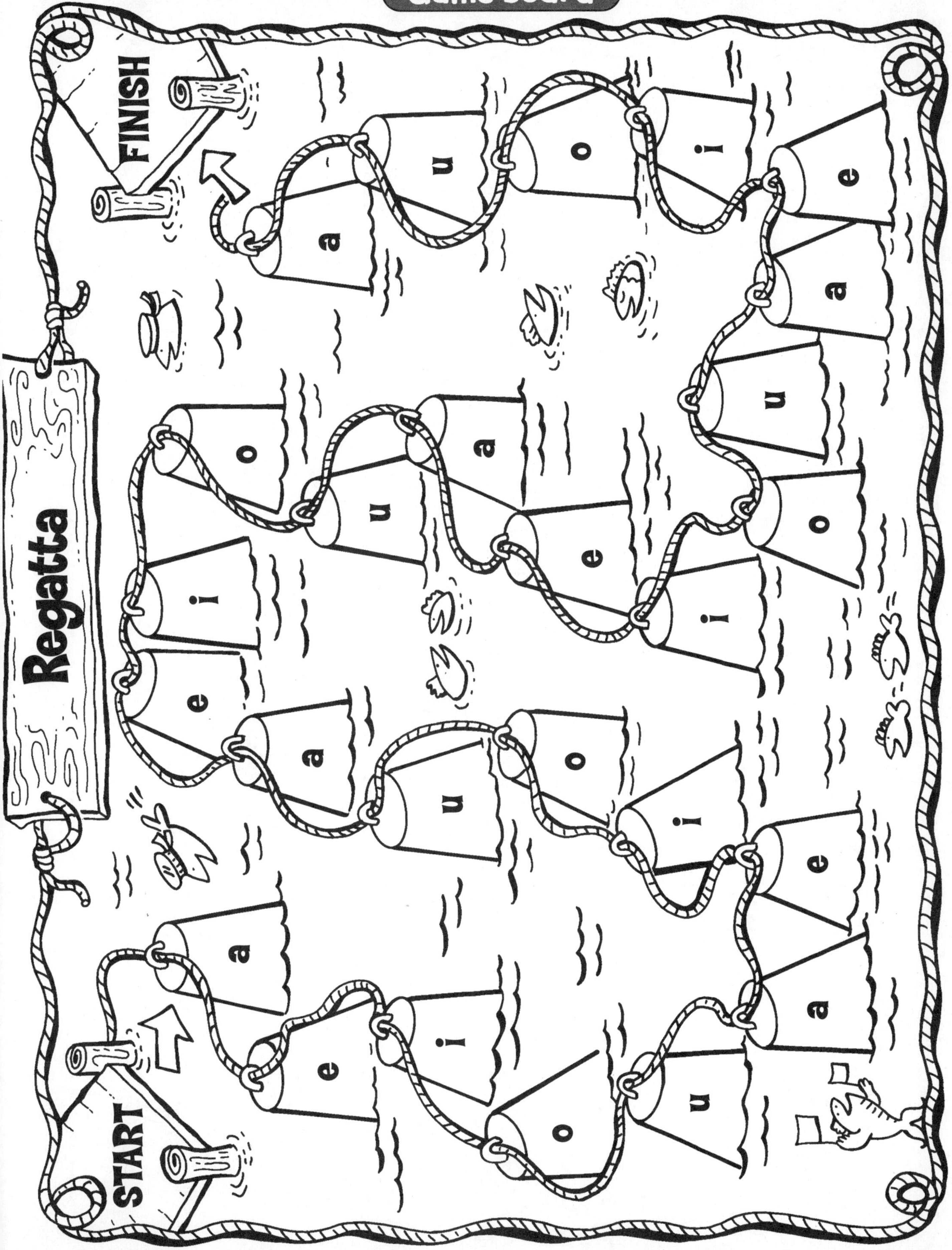

FINISH

Regatta

START

a u o i e

a

u

o

i o

a

e i

o

u a

e

i

a

e o

u

a

BOAT MARKERS

leaf	tree	cheese
cake	feet	tape
cone	tube	boat
hose	soap	bone
toe	bike	kite

nose

coat

tie

cane

rake

cube

snake

vase

glue

pie

flute

hive

nine

rope

ice

mule

seal

bee

LOSE A TURN

GO BACK TO START

TAKE ANOTHER TURN

Snapshot

Skill

Identifying short-vowel sounds

Players

2 to 4

Object

To be the first player to fill up a Photo Album

Materials

- Snapshot game board (page 25)
- Photo Word cards (page 26)
- Photo Album game card for each player (page 27)
- Number cube (page 27)
- Camera markers (page 26)

How to Play

1. Shuffle the Photo Word cards and place them in spaces around the Snapshot game board (excluding the "Watch the Birdie!" corners).

2. Each player places a Camera marker on one corner of the board. Players take turns rolling the number cube to determine how many spaces to move clockwise around the game board. If a player can identify the short-vowel sound in the picture he or she lands on, the player can take that Photo card and place it on the correct vowel in his or her Photo Album. Only one photo is allowed on each vowel space.

3. The first player to fill in all the spaces in his or her Photo Album wins.

Variation:

Delete one space and cover up the other letters on the Photo Album game card before reproducing. Assign each game card one letter (for instance, all E's). Players fill up their Photo Albums with pictures that have the same vowel sound as that letter.

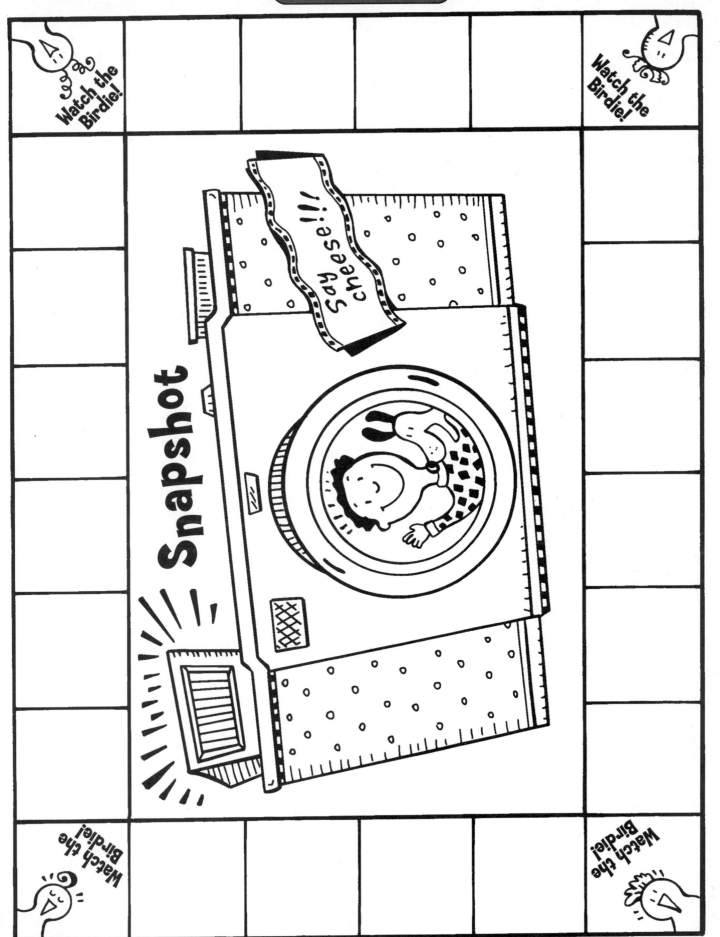

Photo Word Cards

CAMERA MARKERS

cat	apple	bat	hat
lock	mop	clock	doll
nest	hen	web	pen
fish	bib	lips	pig
sun	duck	rug	bus

Photo Album Game Card

A E I

O U

NUMBER CUBE

GLUE
GLUE 2 GLUE
1 1 2 1 GLUE
GLUE 2 GLUE
GLUE

Alphabet Soup

Skill
Forming short words

Players
2 to 4

Object
To form words out of Alphabet Noodle Cards and collect the most Crackers

Materials
- Soup Bowl game board (page 29)
- Alphabet Noodle cards (page 30)
- Number cube (page 30)
- 10 Cracker markers (page 30)

How to Play

1. Spread the Alphabet Noodle cards faceup in the middle of the Soup Bowl. Place the Crackers next to the Bowl.

2. Players take turns rolling the number cube to determine how many Alphabet Noodle cards to use to make a word. For example, if a player rolls a 3, he or she tries to make a three-letter word using the Alphabet Noodle cards.

3. If a player forms a word, he or she collects one Cracker. A word may be used only once. The player returns the Noodle cards to the Bowl.

4. Play continues until all the crackers are gone. The player with the most Crackers wins.

Variation:
Turn the Alphabet Noodle cards facedown. Players take turns drawing the cards until none remain, then use their cards to make words in the Bowl. The player to use the most cards wins.

Soup Bowl

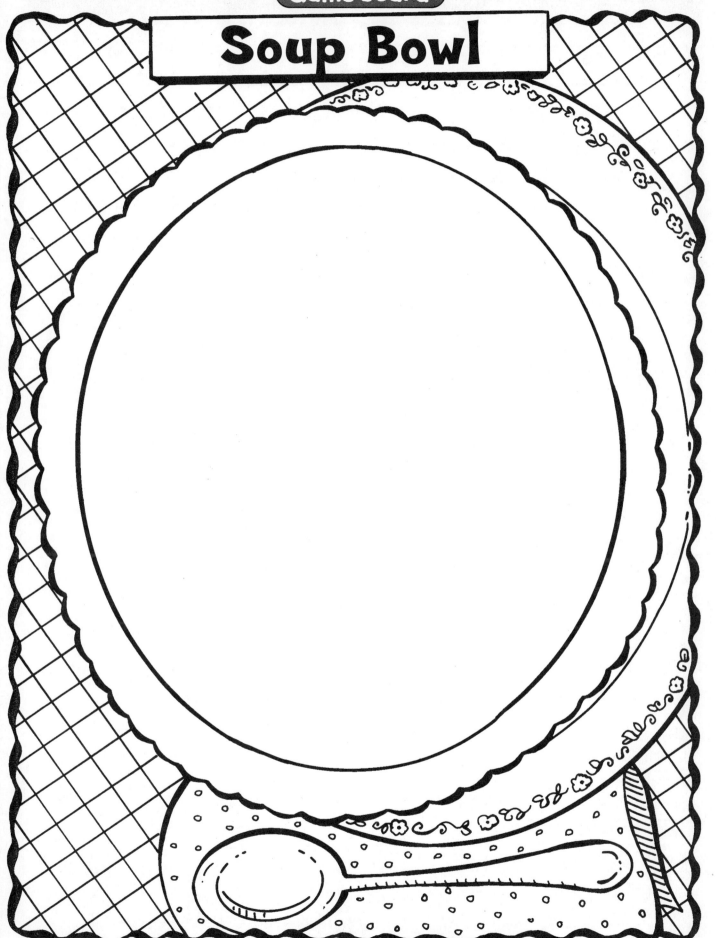

a	a	b	b	c	c
d	d	e	e	f	f
g	g	h	h	i	i
j	j	k	k	l	l
m	m	n	n	o	o
p	p	q	q	r	r
s	s	t	t	u	u
v	v	w	w	x	x
y	y	z	z	a	e
i	o	a	e	i	o

CRACKER MARKERS

NUMBER CUBE

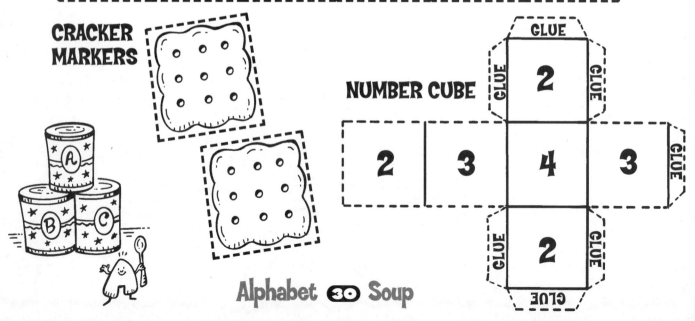

Alphabet 30 Soup

Bug in a Rug

Skill
Matching rhyming words

Players
2 to 4

Object
To match rhyming words and collect the most Bugs

Materials
- Bug in a Rug game board (page 32)
- Word cards (pages 33–34)
- Number cube (page 34)
- 10 Bug markers (page 34)

How to Play

1. Place the Bugs under the game board. Shuffle the Word cards and stack them facedown next to the game board.

2. Deal three cards to each player, keeping the cards facedown. Players take turns rolling the number cube to determine how many Word cards to take from the stack. If a player rolls the bug on the cube, he or she shouts, "Bug in a Rug." Players then turn over their cards and try to match each word to a rhyming picture on the game board. For example, a player may put "cat" on the "hat" space. The first player to match all of his or her pictures takes a Bug from under the game board.

3. Remove the cards from the game board and reshuffle them to start a new game. Play continues until all the Bugs have been removed. The player with the most Bugs wins.

Variation:
For a creative writing activity, turn all the Word cards facedown. Students take turns selecting four cards, then try to create a rhyming verse using those words.

Bug in a Rug

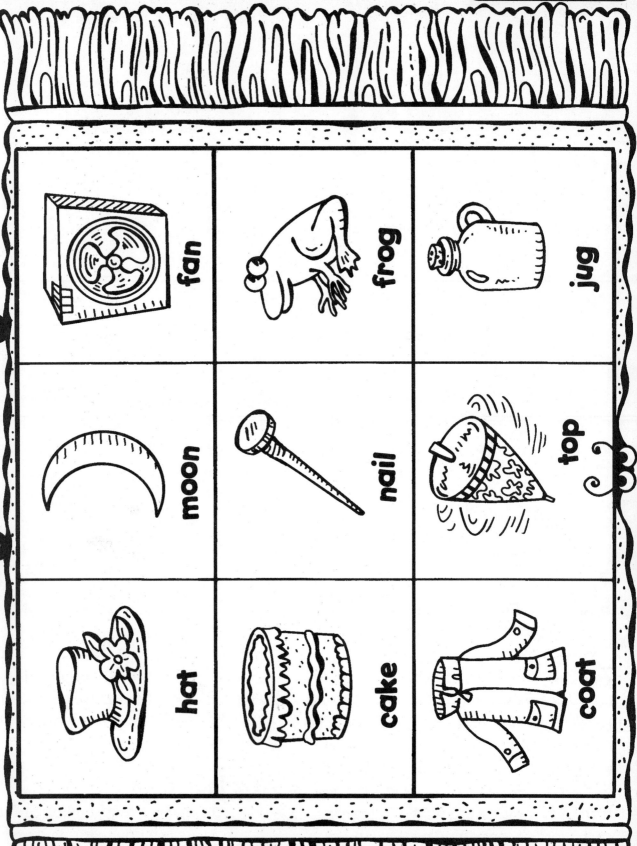

fan

frog

jug

moon

nail

top

hat

cake

coat

rug	cat	bug	oat
rake	lake	snake	hog
man	pail	pan	mug
hop	sail	mail	log
stop	mop	can	goat
spoon	June	noon	bat

boat | rat | dog

Game Pieces

BUG MARKERS

NUMBER CUBE

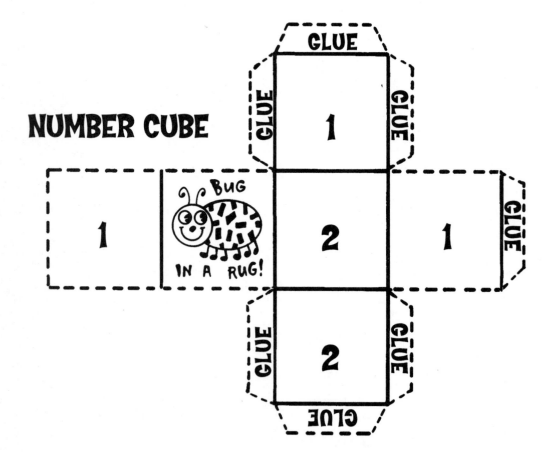

GLUE

GLUE   1   GLUE

1   BUG IN A RUG!   2   1   GLUE

GLUE   2   GLUE

GLUE

Stop and Go

Skill
Matching opposites

Players
2, plus a Traffic Cop

Object
To name the opposite of a word and be the first player to get his or her School Bus to school

Materials
- Stop and Go game board (page 36)
- Opposite Word cards (page 37)
- Traffic Light cube (page 37)
- School Bus markers (page 37)

How to Play

1. Color three of the circles on the Traffic Light cube green and three red. Shuffle the Opposite cards and stack them facedown next to the Traffic Cop.

2. Each player places a School Bus marker at START. Players take turns rolling the cube. If the cube shows a red circle, the player may not move. If the cube shows a green circle, the player advances one space. The Traffic Cop picks an Opposite Word card and reads the first word aloud. If the player can name that word's opposite (in parentheses), he or she may roll the cube again. The player's turn ends when he or she rolls a red or answers incorrectly.

3. Play continues until one player's Bus reaches the school (FINISH) and wins.

Variation:
Instead of Opposite cards, make cards with questions the players can answer about themselves. For instance: How do you spell your first name? What is your last name? What is your teacher's name? What room are you in?

Game Board

Stop and Go

School

FINISH

Bus Stop

START

BUS MARKERS

TRAFFIC LIGHT CUBE

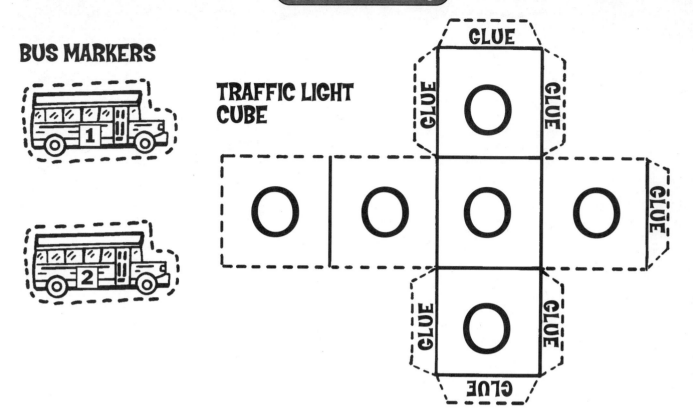

open (close)	**stop** (go)	**up** (down)	**on** (off)	**in** (out)	**big** (little)
tall (short)	**young** (old)	**night** (day)	**run** (walk)	**sit** (stand)	**happy** (sad)
hot (cold)	**yes** (no)	**fast** (slow)	**pretty** (ugly)	**bad** (good)	**black** (white)
fat (thin)	**left** (right)	**laugh** (cry)	**win** (lose)	**sharp** (dull)	**over** (under)
boy (girl)	**sweet** (sour)	**full** (empty)	**rainy** (sunny)	**shout** (whisper)	**high** (low)

Pairs of Pears

Skill
Matching homophones

Players
2

Object
To match cards with similar-sounding words and collect the most pairs

Materials
• Pear cards (pages 39–40)

How to Play

1. Shuffle the Pear cards and deal five cards to each player. Stack the remaining cards facedown with the top card faceup next to the stack. This is the discard pile.

2. Players take turns either drawing a card from the stack or taking the top card from the discard pile. When a player can match two homophones, he or she places the pair faceup on the table. Players must always discard a card after picking a new one.

3. Play continues until one player has matched all of his or her cards.

Variation:

Deal five cards each to two players. Put the remaining cards in a stack facedown on the table and turn over one card for the discard pile. Players take turns asking each other for a card needed to make a pair. If the other player has the card, he or she must hand it over. If not, he or she says, "Pick a Pear," and the first player either chooses a card from the stack or takes the top card from the discard pile. A player must always discard a card after picking a new one.

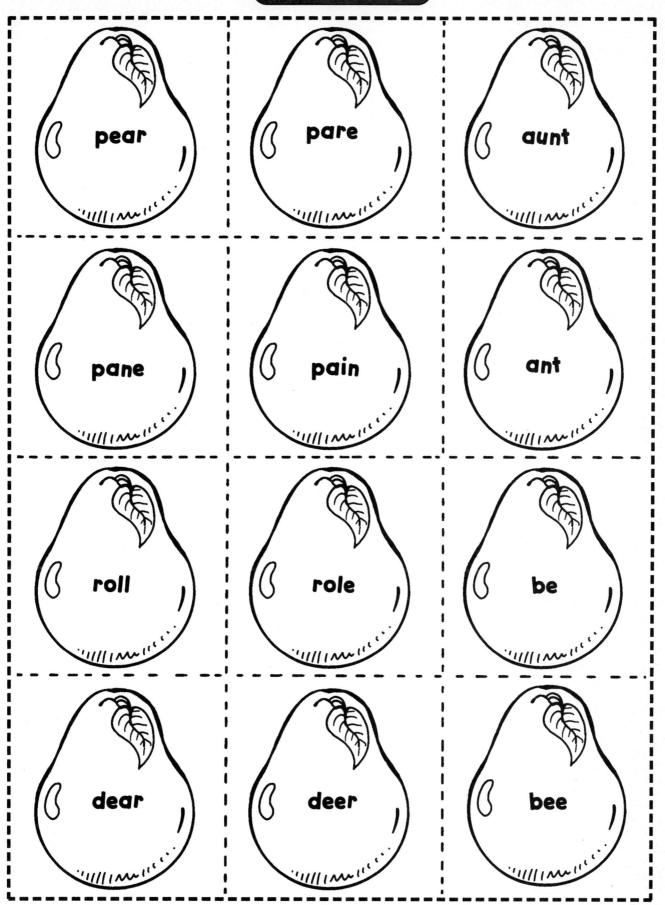

pear

pare

aunt

pane

pain

ant

roll

role

be

dear

deer

bee

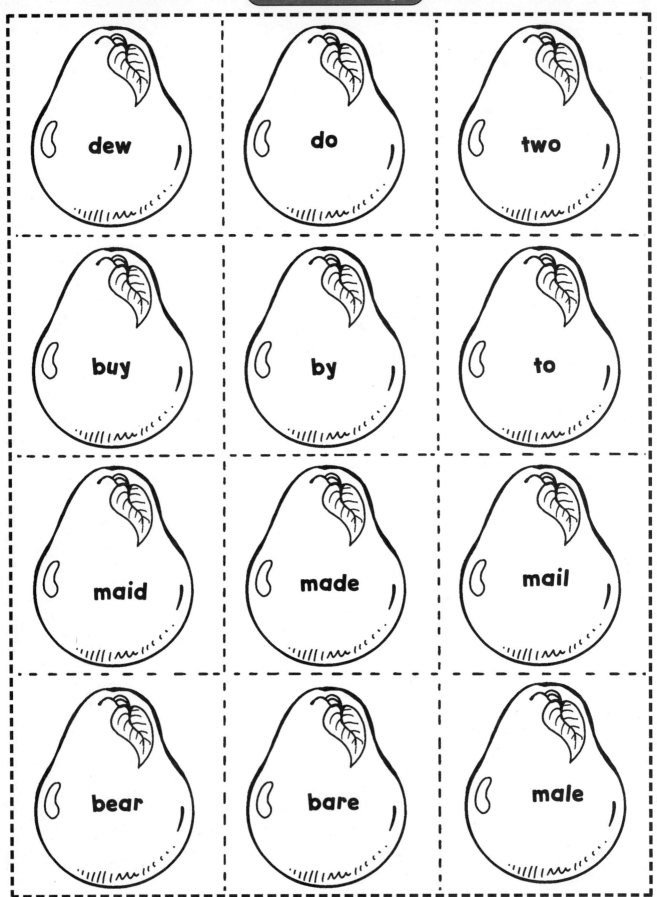

dew

do

two

buy

by

to

maid

made

mail

bear

bare

male

Goofy Glasses

Skill
Identifying basic sight words

Players
2 to 4

Object
To match word cards with the correct picture cards and collect the most pairs

Materials
- Goofy Glasses game board for each player (page 42)
- Lens cards (pages 42–43)

How to Play

1. Provide each player with a Goofy Glasses game board. Spread the Lens cards facedown on the table.

2. Players take turns turning over two cards at a time. If the player chooses matching word and picture cards, he or she places the cards in his or her Glasses and says the word correctly. The player keeps the pair of cards.

3. Play continues until all the cards have been matched. The player with the most pairs wins.

Variation:
At the beginning of the school year, help students get to know each other by writing their names on Lens cards and gluing their photos to other cards. Play the game as above. You can also use pictures of school personnel (principal, librarian, art teacher).

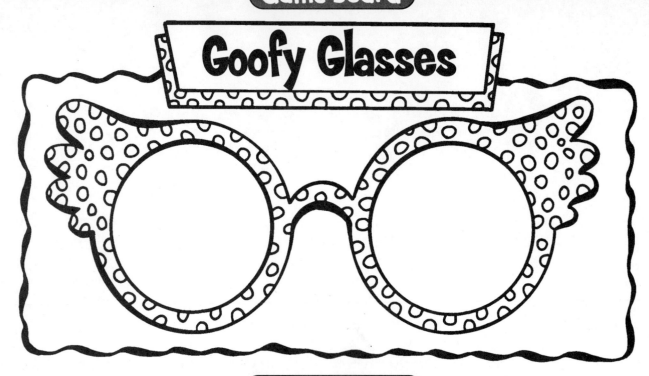

Goofy Glasses

- - - Game Cards - - -

book	cat	fish	dog
pie	bee	cup	boat
clock	kite	pig	hat

bat

bus

duck

sun

Milkshake

Skill
Creating compound words

Players
2 to 4, plus a Scorekeeper

Object
To form compound words and be the first player to earn 10 points

Materials
- Compound cubes (page 45)
- Large paper cup with lid
- Paper and pencil (for the Scorekeeper)

How to Play

1. Place the Compound cubes in the cup and secure the lid.

2. Players take turns shaking the cup, removing the lid, and tossing the cubes onto the table. The player must try to make up one or more compound words using the words on the cubes. The Scorekeeper awards one point for each word created.

3. The first player to earn 10 points wins.

Variation:
Use the compound cubes for story starters. Have a student toss the cubes and create a story using the words that land faceup.

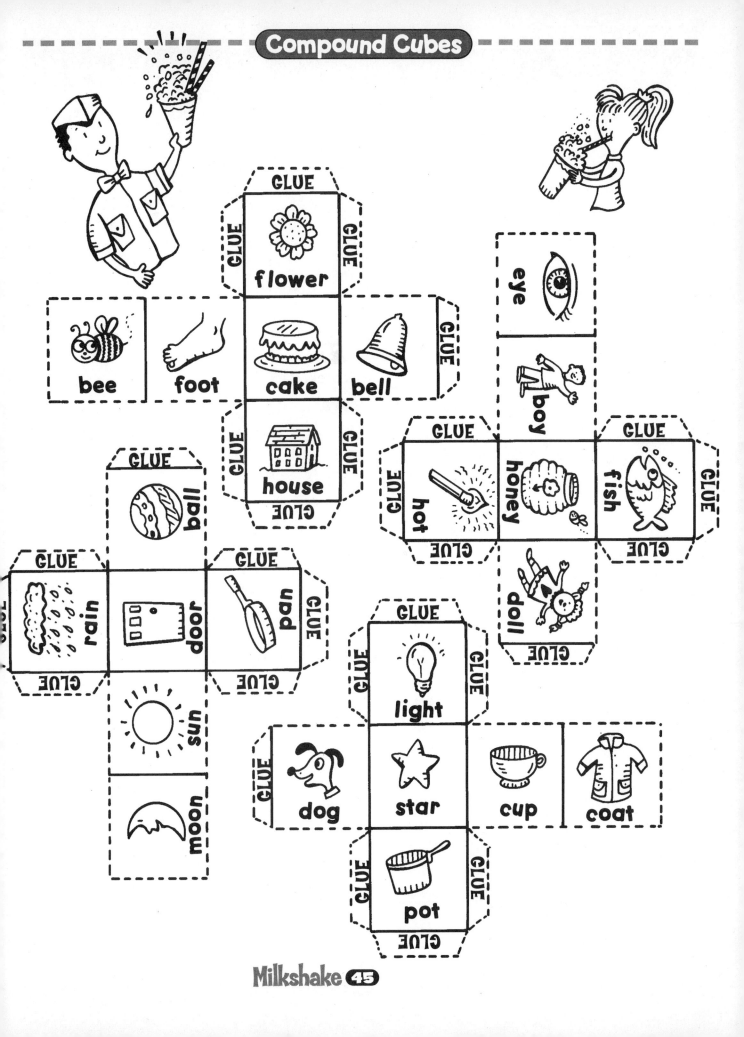

GLUE

flower

GLUE

GLUE

bee foot cake bell

GLUE

GLUE

house

GLUE

eye

boy

GLUE GLUE

hot honey fish

GLUE

doll

GLUE

GLUE

ball

GLUE

GLUE

rain door pan

GLUE

GLUE GLUE

sun

moon

GLUE

light

GLUE

dog star cup coat

GLUE GLUE

pot

GLUE

Feed the Dog

Skill
Using correct punctuation

Players
2 to 4

Object
To match the sentences on Bone cards with the correct punctuation
on the game board and be the first player to get rid of all his or her Bone cards

Materials
- Feed the Dog game board (page 47)
- Bone cards (page 48)

- -

How to Play

1. Shuffle the Bone cards and deal them to each player. All players should have the same number of cards.

2. Players take turns reading a Bone card and deciding which type of punctuation comes at the end of the sentence. Then they place the Bone in the mouth of the dog with the correct punctuation mark.

3. If a player is correct, his or her Bone stays in the dog's mouth. If not, the player takes back the Bone and waits for his or her next turn.

4. The first player to get rid of all his or her Bone cards wins.

Variation:
Challenge students to write their own sentences on blank Bone cards.

Feed the Dog

question mark ?

? ? ? ? ?

exclamation point !

! ! ! ! !

period •

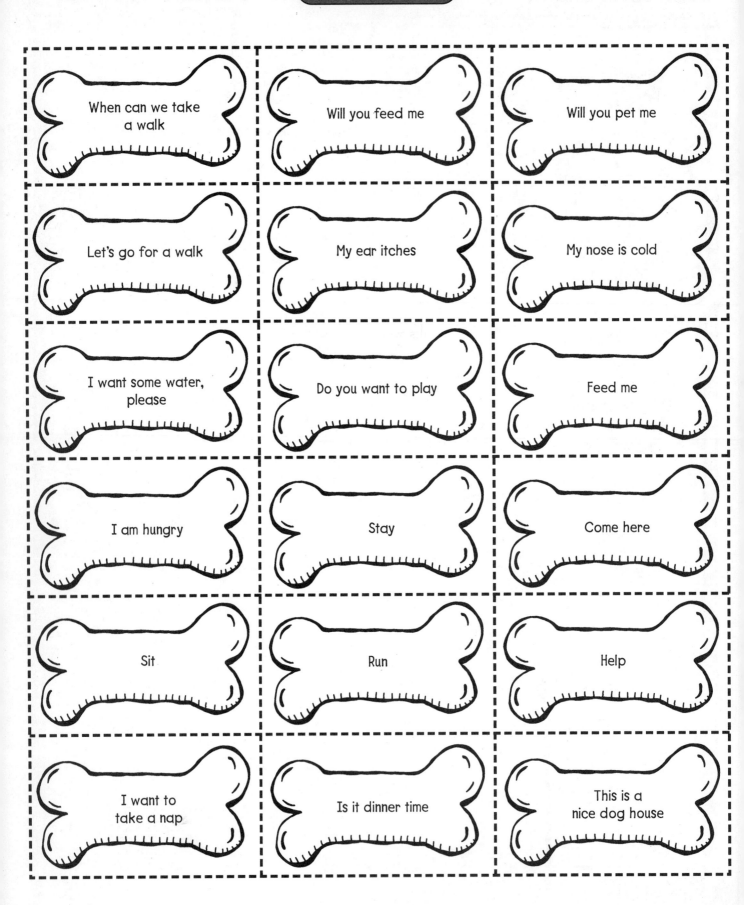

When can we take a walk

Will you feed me

Will you pet me

Let's go for a walk

My ear itches

My nose is cold

I want some water, please

Do you want to play

Feed me

I am hungry

Stay

Come here

Sit

Run

Help

I want to take a nap

Is it dinner time

This is a nice dog house